Quote Octopus
Melbourne, Victoria, 3053
Australia
www.quoteoctopus.com

I hate to advocate drugs, alcohol, violence, or insanity to anyone, but they've always worked for me.

Hunter S. Thompson

Anyway, no drug, not even alcohol, causes the fundamental ills of society. If we're looking for the source of our troubles, we shouldn't test people for drugs, we should test them for stupidity, ignorance, greed and love of power.

P. J. O'Rourke

Herb is the healing of a nation, alcohol is the destruction.

Bob Marley

Alcohol may be man's worst enemy, but the bible says love your enemy.

Frank Sinatra

My peers, lately, have found companionship through means of intoxication - it makes them sociable. I, however, cannot force myself to use drugs to cheat on my loneliness - it is all that I have - and when the drugs and alcohol dissipate, will be all that my peers have as well.

Franz Kafka

Alcohol is like love. The first kiss is magic, the second is intimate, the third is routine. After that you take the girl's clothes off.

Raymond Chandler

Let me be the first to tell you, drinking alcohol is the worst thing to do in cold weather. Hot soup is the best because the process of digesting food helps to warm you up.

Morgan Freeman

Alcohol is the anesthesia by which we endure the operation of life.

George Bernard Shaw

There are six components of wellness: proper weight and diet, proper exercise, breaking the smoking habit, control of alcohol, stress management and periodic exams.

Kenneth H. Cooper

Every form of addiction is bad, no matter whether the narcotic be alcohol or morphine or idealism.

Carl Jung

Young people can get very discouraged and get hooked on drugs or on alcohol because of problems they perceive as insurmountable. It is important that they realize a mistake need not ruin their future, but they must also know that not everything in life is a bed of roses.

Maureen Forrester

I have taken more out of alcohol than alcohol has taken out of me.

Winston Churchill

There are hundreds of millions of gun owners in this country, and not one of them will have an accident today. The only misuse of guns comes in environments where there are drugs, alcohol, bad parents, and undisciplined children. Period.

Ted Nugent

I wish all teenagers can filter through songs instead of turning to drugs and alcohol.

Taylor Swift

Alcohol gives you infinite patience for stupidity.

Sammy Davis, Jr.

My rule of life prescribed as an absolutely sacred rite smoking cigars and also the drinking of alcohol before, after and if need be during all meals and in the intervals between them.

Winston Churchill

I'm very serious about no alcohol, no drugs. Life is too beautiful.

Jim Carrey

I was always going to church with my mom, dad and sister. I was literally raised under the godly influence both at home and church. There was no alcohol and no smoking at our house. That was the way a Bowden was supposed to live. My dad always told me to represent the Bowden name in a respectful manner.

Bobby Bowden

Here's to alcohol: the cause of, and answer to, all of life's problems.

Matt Groening

I am more afraid of alcohol than of all the bullets of the enemy.

Stonewall Jackson

You got to realise that when I was 20 years old, I had a house, a Mercedes, a Corvette and a million dollars in the bank before I could buy alcohol legally.

Dr. Dre

The sway of alcohol over mankind is unquestionably due to its power to stimulate the mystical faculties of human nature, usually crushed to earth by the cold facts and dry criticisms of the sober hour.

William James

Negative freedom is freedom from - freedom from oppression, whether it's a colonial power or addiction to alcohol oppressing you. You need to be freed from negative freedom. Positive freedom is freedom for, freedom to be. And that's what's routinely ignored today.

Os Guinness

When I have an idea, I turn down the flame, as if it were a little alcohol stove, as low as it will go. Then it explodes and that is my idea.

Ernest Hemingway

I don't even drink! I can't stand the taste of alcohol. Every New Year's Eve I try one drink and every time it makes me feel sick. So I don't touch booze - I'm always the designated driver.

Kim Kardashian

Avoid using cigarettes, alcohol, and drugs as alternatives to being an interesting person.

Marilyn vos Savant

Minimum sales prices for alcohol are a startlingly bad idea. As with excise duties, the effects are regressive.

Nigel Farage

Such lifestyle factors such as cigarette smoking, excessive alcohol consumption, little physical activity and low dietary calcium intake are risk factors for osteoporosis as well as for many other non-communicable diseases.

Gro Harlem Brundtland

Alcohol doesn't console, it doesn't fill up anyone's psychological gaps, all it replaces is the lack of God. It doesn't comfort man. On the contrary, it encourages him in his folly, it transports him to the supreme regions where he is master of his own destiny.

Marguerite Duras

Hindered by asthma since I was six weeks old, I had begun experimenting with my diet and discovered a disquieting correlation. When I stopped eating the normal American diet of sugar, fats, alcohol, chemicals, and additives, I felt better. I could breathe freely. When I tried to sneak in a hamburger and a Coke, my body rebelled.

Paul Hawken

The Teen Challenge ministry was born out of those humble early days of ministry. It now includes over 500 drug and alcohol rehab centers around the world, even in Muslim countries. These include homes for girls and women addicts and alcoholics, all which are reaching many.

David Wilkerson

Another method of eating burning coals employs small balls of burned cotton in a dish of burning alcohol.

Harry Houdini

I don't like alcohol, but I still like to mess around with other stuff occasionally. I think it's important I take mushrooms and acid. They're certainly not addictive, so I can't rule that out.

Evan Dando

In England, it's a rare thing to see a player smoking but, all in all, I prefer that to an alcoholic. The relationship with alcohol is a real problem in English football and, in the short term, it's much more harmful to a sportsman. It weakens the body, which becomes more susceptible to injury.

Alex Ferguson

Our national drug is alcohol. We tend to regard the use any other drug with special horror.

William S. Burroughs

But when alcohol comes in, start running. Because there's a demon there, and it goes back to her childhood.

David Gest

When Prohibition was first enacted in 1920, most people stockpiled alcohol, thinking they'd have enough to last them for years. By 1923, that was starting to run out, so your average person started to rely more and more on criminals.

Terence Winter

There'd never been a more advantageous time to be a criminal in America than during the 13 years of Prohibition. At a stroke, the American government closed down the fifth largest industry in the United States - alcohol production - and just handed it to criminals - a pretty remarkable thing to do.

Bill Bryson

Millions of people die every day. Everyone's got to go sometime. I've came by this particular tumor honestly. If you smoke, which I did for many years very heavily with occasional interruption, and if you use alcohol, you make yourself a candidate for it in your sixties.

Christopher Hitchens

I'm a big fan of the effects of alcohol.

Peter Steele

It is critical that parents and other trusted adults initiate conversations with kids about underage drinking well in advance of the first time they are faced with a decision regarding alcohol.

Xavier Becerra

I got sober. I stopped killing myself with alcohol. I began to think: 'Wait a minute - if I can stop doing this, what are the possibilities?' And slowly it dawned on me that it was maybe worth the risk.

Craig Ferguson

That's all drugs and alcohol do, they cut off your emotions in the end.

Ringo Starr

It was my Uncle George who discovered that alcohol was a food well in advance of modern medical thought.

P. G. Wodehouse

No other human being, no woman, no poem or music, book or painting can replace alcohol in its power to give man the illusion of real creation.

Marguerite Duras

Alcohol decimated the working class and so many people.

Martin Scorsese

Drugs, alcohol and ego. They are a bad mix.

Don Dokken

The presidents of colleges have to have some courage to step forward. You can't limit alcohol in college sports, you have to get rid of it.

Dean Smith

If they took all the drugs, nicotine, alcohol and caffeine off the market for six days, they'd have to bring out the tanks to control you.

Dick Gregory

Craft brewers are committed to promoting the safe and moderate consumption of their beverage, and work closely with their communities to prevent underage drinking and alcohol abuse.

Sherwood Boehlert

I'm sure there have been a lot of boys I've chased over the years that has been fueled by alcohol and stupidity. But that's kind of how things happen - sometimes you have to do something really stupid, and sometimes it works out, and sometimes you fall flat on your face.

Noel Wells

I hate the taste of alcohol. When I'm drinking, I'm drinking Red Bull.

Paris Hilton

Mankind: A quality of life upgrade is available to each and every one of you. It should give you a quality of life upgrade, which means no drugs, no alcohol, no fast food - unless, of course, it's a mallard.

Ted Nugent

Being smarter gives you a tailwind throughout life. People who are more intelligent earn more, live longer, get divorced less, are less likely to get addicted to alcohol and tobacco, and their children live longer.

Steven Pinker

Somebody said to me this morning, 'To what do you attribute your longevity?' I don't know. I mean, I couldn't have planned my life out better. By all accounts I should be dead! The abuse I put my body through: the drugs, the alcohol, the lifestyle I've lived the last 30 years!

Ozzy Osbourne

Some parents let their kids sleep at other people's houses, where they drink alcohol, watch TV for hours and God knows what else. But if you say you have to get all A's and practice the violin for two hours, then they consider that abusive. That upsets me.

Amy Chua

I am fussy, about my diet and straining my voice. I know, sounds a bit over the top. But I'm not as bad as I used to be.

These days I don't drink alcohol for five days before a show - very dehydrating for the vocal cords, and all that acid reflux. I used to ban it for a fortnight. Nightmare.

Katherine Jenkins

I do like to have fun. I don't need alcohol to have fun.

Rima Fakih

Some people recovering from drugs or alcohol stay with the programs indefinitely, making the recovery program their family, a long-term source of attention rewards.

Keith Henson

Lucy Mercedes Martinez, my mother, was probably my first mentor. She really tried to take care of me in spite of myself, and in spite of her own struggles with alcohol. She was an immigrant who had never finished school. But she was also a Renaissance woman who read voraciously. She spoke several languages.

Richard Carmona

I don't know of any issues associated with alcohol before flight.

Ellen Ochoa

I don't like dirty. That's why I hate cigarettes. A little bit of alcohol is O.K., but no drugs. And I like to sleep alone because I wake up, I walk around, I bring my computer with me to bed, I have a great time.

Jean Pigozzi

Man seeks to escape himself in myth, and does so by any means at his disposal. Drugs, alcohol, or lies. Unable to withdraw into himself, he disguises himself. Lies and inaccuracy give him a few moments of comfort.

Jean Cocteau

Alcohol is necessary for a man so that he can have a good opinion of himself, undisturbed be the facts.

Finley Peter Dunne

Alcohol is a very patient drug. It will wait for the alcoholic to pick it up one more time.

Mercedes McCambridge

Alcohol is barren. The words a man speaks in the night of drunkenness fade like the darkness itself at the coming of day.

Marguerite Duras

As women slowly gain power, their values and priorities are reshaping the agenda. A multitude of studies show that when women control the family funds, they generally spend more on health, nutrition, and education - and less on alcohol and cigarettes.

Dee Dee Myers

Alcohol, tobacco, and pharmaceutical drugs are legal, but they can hurt a lot of people.

Ziggy Marley

If you substitute marijuana for tobacco and alcohol, you'll add eight to 24 years to your life.

Jack Herer

'Comfy,' that's one of the worst words! I just picture a woman feeling bad, with a big bottle of alcohol, really puffy. It's really depressing, but she likes her life because she has comfortable clogs.

Christian Louboutin

I'm glad now, at age 66, that I never used alcohol or tobacco... I've buried a lot of friends who used tobacco or alcohol.

Jerry Falwell

I do like beer, but lately I've started drinking non-alcoholic beer and I like the taste of it and I don't get the alcohol, so that's a good alternative also.

Mike Ditka

I think your alcohol intake has to change. You know, usually a big person feels they can drink anything they want to and as much as they want to and I've cut that way back.

Mike Ditka

Everybody needs a way out of that pain. Many people choose drugs and alcohol. Some people obsessively exercise or develop strange dietary habits, which is what I did. At least it got me toward a path of healthier living.

Mariel Hemingway

I think, at a certain point, it's better for women not to have any alcohol because it can make your face, breasts and midsection get very bloated.

Sharon Stone

Kids are going to try drugs and alcohol; that's part of society.

Jamie Lee Curtis

I'm not really the party person. I don't 'become myself' once I'm drunk. I don't use alcohol to be happy.

Jessie J

Just as the process of repealing national alcohol prohibition began with individual states repealing their own prohibition laws, so individual states must now take the initiative with respect to repealing marijuana prohibition laws.

George Soros

According to the National Institute on Drug Abuse, the first use of alcohol typically begins at age 12.

Xavier Becerra

I had such a wonderful life before drugs and alcohol abuse. I've got that life back now and plan to keep it. Maybe I had to go through what I did to get to this point, to appreciate this life more.

Harvey Martin

One day my wife went and saw the accountant and said she's pulling the plug. She said you guys are done. I said, how bad can it be? 10 grand? She said you're not even close. It came out to almost $50,000 in alcohol for two months.

Zakk Wylde

Alcohol is a big part of high school. I went through my little phase. I don't know one high schooler that doesn't.

Shailene Woodley

Chess: It's like alcohol. It's a drug. I have to control it, or it could overwhelm me. I have a regular Monday night game at my home, and I do play a little online.

Charles Krauthammer

But there is no withdrawal, but with tobacco there is terrible withdrawal, it is almost impossible for a lot of people. I did , I went cold turkey, they never had any patches in those days but grass was not difficult, alcohol not difficult, but tobacco - oh my god.

Larry Hagman

I think people tend to see the bigger point, which is maybe not fitting in and feeling like you didn't have the childhood that you expected you would have, or that you felt lonely or struggled with drugs and alcohol or just that you were able to achieve your dreams.

Augusten Burroughs

I don't smoke marijuana anymore. I don't drink. Marijuana is a handicap. So is alcohol. Alcohol is a terrible handicap. But in spite of being a handicap, it shouldn't be criminal.

Gary Johnson

I'm not a big drinking person and hardly ever have alcohol. Perhaps it's not sweet enough for my sweet tooth.

Dawn French

The good news is that parents are the leading influence on kids' decision not to drink alcohol.

Xavier Becerra

I'm a germ-phobe when I meet a lot of people or shake a lot of hands. I always have hand sanitizer and alcohol swabs so I can sort of go back and forth between the two.

Mandy Moore

As a civil servant in charge of the government's Strategy Unit, I brought in many people from outside government, including academia and science, to work in the unit, dissecting and solving complex problems from GM crops to alcohol, nuclear proliferation to schools reform.

Geoff Mulgan

People in the business will stay with you through drugs and alcohol and divorces and insanity and everything else, but you have a failure, pal, and they don't want to know nothing about you!

Don Johnson

I just don't drink alcohol. I never have; I never will.

Kat Graham

According to Teenage Research Unlimited, 51 percent of 13-15 year olds say they will be faced with making a decision regarding alcohol in the next three months.

Xavier Becerra

So at the end of the day, our number 1 goal, our top priority, is to motivate American youngsters to reject the abuse of illegal drugs, tobacco and alcohol. All three of them are illegal behaviors.

Barry McCaffrey

We put more emphasis on who can drive a car than on who can be a parent. And I think there ought to be mandatory parenting classes starting in high school, and you should have to have a license to be able to be a parent to explain that you don't give alcohol to kids.

Dale Archer

There's so much fear involved in trying to do something you don't know how to do that drugs and alcohol can become a big part of your life if you have an addictive personality or are very unsure, which most songwriters are.

Barry Mann

Part of treatment for drugs and alcohol is you abstain from these, but with eating disorders you can't abstain from food so the treatment is longer than drugs and alcohol.

Carre Otis

My life was a complete catatrophe. I was very, very sick from drugs and alcohol.

Trey Anastasio

Drugs and alcohol can be so destructive.

Kyan Douglas

Alcohol is the cause of all my problems.

Jayson Williams

I think once I made up my mind that I was allergic to alcohol, and that's what I learned, it made sense to me. And I think it was kind of pointed out that you know if you were allergic to strawberries, you wouldn't eat strawberries. And that made sense to me.

Betty Ford

Taking B12 is the price of getting to be vegan, the way wearing a helmet is the price of getting to ride a motorcycle and giving up alcohol for nine months is the price of getting to have a baby.

Victoria Moran

In reality, we can prove that the incidents of drug, alcohol abuse and violence have dropped dramatically among professional athletes - but the problem is it would be impossible to convince than fans, because of what they read on the AP wire.

Leigh Steinberg

The last show we played, I was straight as a die. It did feel weird not to be hiding behind alcohol or dope, but being focused was... good.

Ron Wood

We'd boil this whisky because we thought that would make it stronger. So we thought we were getting drunk, but in fact there'd be no alcohol left in it.

Neneh Cherry

And I have always told the patients when I talk to them. When they come around and say, 'What will you have to drink? Oh that's right you don't drink.' Just speak up and say, 'Of course I drink. But I just don't drink alcohol.'

Betty Ford

I never did drugs and I can't really drink because I have zero tolerance for alcohol, so my vice became women. I was never faithful to most of them.

Scott Baio

I work very hard to keep on an even keel as far as alcohol is concerned.

Trisha Goddard

The stated mission at the time was simply to use the influence of the entertainment industry to do an accurate portrayal of drug and alcohol abuse. We all admit that we're not trying to censor anybody.

Gerald McRaney

And then you have the responsibility and the duty of being good examples to youngsters, not smoke, training hard, go to bed early, don't drink alcohol, don't take drugs, it's very important to have a policy for educating against doping.

Alberto Juantorena

But in my college years it got to the point where my friends and I didn't do anything without consuming a massive amount of alcohol before we went anywhere or did anything, and you know that.

Jim Coleman

We used to drink an awful lot of alcohol.

Bill Bruford

Allowing your kids to watch TV doesn't have to mean they have no choice but to see commercials for junk food and alcohol.

Charlie Ergen

I don't want to get in a big, long discussion about right and wrong, but our company has been working on the issue of underage drinking and alcohol abuse for a long time. I've been outspoken about it.

Pete Coors

My character had been in the chair for seven years. He had gone through his anger, depression, drug and alcohol abuse. He had gone through everything, now he was up, he was happy, he was filled with his dream.

Gregory Hines

When I drank, I had a very different attitude towards my playing. It was sloppier but I kind of liked it that way. It was like the alcohol was telling my mind what to do.

Mick Mars

I would never have discovered alcohol.

David Strickland

But you can count the dead bodies from alcohol, tobacco, and legal pharmaceuticals by the millions.

Jack Herer

With such compelling information, the question is why haven't we been able to do more to prevent the crisis of underage drinking? The answer is: the alcohol industry.

Lucille Roybal-Allard

A good margarita, a good red wine, I like expensive alcohol, but not a lot of it. I don't like to throw up.

Denise Richards

In my private life, I'm not around any drugs or alcohol.

Penn Jillette

I worry about the kids who have too much. As a parent living in a so-called good neighborhood with children who went to private high school, I found myself spending much time in parent groups worrying about alcohol, unsupervised parties, and parents not being parents.

Marian Wright Edelman

I know I was an alcoholic because I was preoccupied whether alcohol was going to be served or not.

Betty Ford

Indians have a big problem with alcohol and drugs. I grew up with an admiration for their culture and was sensitive to their problems.

Kirstie Alley

We tax air passengers like cigarettes and alcohol - we impose sin taxes on travellers.

Gordon Bethune

The secret to everything for me is doing yoga every day. It does do nice things for your body, but it also kind of calms you down and chills you out. Other than that, I don't really drink alcohol and I always take my makeup off at night!

Kate Beckinsale

My second marriage had a lot to do with alcohol.

Mercedes McCambridge

Being raised Catholic in a pressure-cooker household besieged by alcohol and bill collectors enforced and heightened a sense of sentry duty in me, the oldest of five children and the one most responsible for keeping everything from capsizing. Wild indulgence was for other people, the non-worriers.

James Wolcott

Our young people are out on the streets looking for parties, a place to dance, looking for a scene. No institutions are providing them with alternatives, fun things to do that don't necessarily have alcohol at the center.

Donna Shalala

I don't really like to drink. I don't like the way alcohol feels or tastes. On occasion I'll do it as a social thing, just to kind of go, 'Hey! I did something with you guys!'

Reggie Watts

I had the taste of the alcohol since I was 11. It allowed me to be clever, charming and to behave outrageously. Acting also allowed me not to be me. So I could indulge every fantasy in this paradise of America.

Malachy McCourt

Writing is the process of finding something to distract you from writing, and of all the helpful distractions - adultery, alcohol and acedia, all of which aided our writing fathers - none can equal the Internet.

Adam Gopnik

At Linfox we have zero tolerance. If any alcohol or drugs are found in any drivers' blood, they are instantly dismissed.

Lindsay Fox

We must do all we can to empower parents and communities to protect our youth and to encourage healthy behavior free from binge drinking and other forms of alcohol abuse.

Jon Corzine

No one will deny that the excessive use of alcohol and alcoholic beverages would do more than any other single factor to make impossible a total war effort.

William Lyon Mackenzie King

The main bone of contention is whether Islamic injunctions are legal or moral categories. When Muslims say Islam commands daily prayers or bans alcohol, are they talking about public obligations that will be enforced by the state or personal ones that will be judged by God?

Mustafa Akyol

It's absolutely absurd to even consider voting on Sunday alcohol sales. I am opposed to alcohol period. It doesn't do anybody any good in the long run. It's a dangerous drug.

John Hunter

Frankly, alcohol leads to a lot of other things when you start drinking at 12-years old. It is a big problem that needs to be addressed. Frankly, the industry has pushed us back and pushed us back.

Zach Wamp

There's nothing like taking two flights when you have a horrible hangover. It's bad when people can see actual alcohol seeping out of your disgusting pores.

Ike Barinholtz

I had a real good thing going for me, and I got sidetracked. It doesn't have to be that way. It doesn't have to be drugs. It doesn't have to be alcohol. That part of my life is over.

Ken Caminiti

I began drinking alcohol at the age of thirteen and gave it up in my fifty sixth year; it was like going straight from puberty to a mid-life crisis.

George Montgomery

Waco was supposed to be a way for the Bureau of Alcohol, Tobacco, and Firearms and the Clinton administration to prove the need for a ban on so-called assault weapons.

Steve Stockman

When I see a serious problem, I try to figure out, my way, how to solve it, how to fix it. When I'm back here in the U.S., I'm speaking, raising funds, and everything for what I do overseas, but at the same time, I speak in schools, colleges, on drugs and alcohol. I come back here and I go into a different fight. But really, it's all related.

Sam Childers

I've never had a drink of alcohol or any drug in my life.

Penn Jillette

I don't smoke and I don't drink alcohol.

Radha Mitchell

If I go out to dinner with you and you order wine, I leave. I won't be around drugs and alcohol at all.

Penn Jillette

After my hip operation, I had to cut out butter, which I loved, and salt. I no longer eat desserts with lots of cream, and I've cut right back on alcohol.

Maeve Binchy

I don't really drink very much, although I have abused alcohol in the past.

Daniel Baldwin

I would say 95% of the time, because you just can't remember your lines if you're drinking alcohol. I would say about 95% of the time it was grape juice or this fake wine, which was horrible.

Thomas Haden Church

Next time we need to be on drugs and have lots of suffering and alcohol abuse going on while recording, I'm kinda picturing a Jerry Lee Lewis session from the mid Seventies.

Jim Diamond

www.ingramcontent.com/pod-product-compliance
Lightning Source LLC
Chambersburg PA
CBHW061944280526
45787CB00004B/1726